READ THIS FIRST

We are educating
the next generation of leaders about
risk management.

Grab your *FREE* Risk and Resilience Tips
for Security Management professionals.

Sign up now at
bit.ly/RiskTakingTipsForLeaders

FLIP THIS RISK®
FOR ENTERPRISE SECURITY

Flip This Risk for Enterprise Security
Industry Experts Share Their Insights About Enterprise
Security Management Risks for Organizations

KAREN HARDY

Flip This Risk® Books
Flipping Risk in Your Favor™
62MediaPublishing.com

Flip This Risk® for Enterprise Security: Industry Experts Share Their Insights About Enterprise Security Management Risks for Organizations

62 Media Publishing is a division of Strategic Leadership Advisors LLC. Visit 62MediaPublishing.com for more information.

ISBN: 978-1-7358786-8-3 (ebook)
ISBN: 978-1-7358786-7-6 (paperback)

Book Cover Design by 62 Media Publishing. Book Interior and ebook Design by Amit Dey. Printed in the United States of America.

Publisher's Cataloging-In-Publication Data
(Prepared by The Donohue Group, Inc.)

Names: Hardy, Karen, 1962- author, editor.
Title: Flip this risk for enterprise security : industry experts share their insights about enterprise security management risks for organizations / Karen Hardy.
Description: First edition. | Upper Marlboro, MD : 62 Media Publishing, a division of Strategic Leadership Advisors, [2021] | Includes bibliographical references.
Identifiers: ISBN 9781735878676 (paperback) | ISBN 9781735878683 (ebook)
Subjects: LCSH: Risk management. | Strategic planning.
Classification: LCC HD61 .H373 2021 (print) | LCC HD61 (ebook) | DDC 658.15/5--dc23

Contents

FLIP THIS RISK®
FOR ENTERPRISE SECURITY

A compilation of stories and industry insights featuring

Daniella Bove-LaMonica
Barrie Burren
RitaBeth Crague
Bridget Guerrero
Karen Hardy
Candace McCabe
Rachael Tovey
Sonia Travi Knowles
Sherry Tucci

Praise for Flip This Risk®

"Congratulations on the work you are doing"

Robert Kaplan
Senior Fellow and Marvin Bower Professor of Leadership
Development, Emeritus - Harvard Business School

"This kind of book series is incredibly important—even inspirational in terms of helping people identify best practices from a non-quantitative perspective. The narratives are incredibly powerful. The conversations with thought leaders and action leaders helps people develop a sense of best practices and models that works for people who are successful --to help you improve your decision-making when you listen to others."

Hersh Shefrin, Professor of Finance
Santa Clara University

Author of *Behavioral Risk Management: Managing the Psychology That Drives Decisions and Influences Operational Risk*

HOW TO USE THIS BOOK

Simplicity is the ultimate sophistication

-Leonardo da Vinci

In risk management there is one thing that holds true: *The simpler the better.* This book represents that mindset. Security management is one of many types of risk organizations manage. The onset of the pandemic introduced both opportunities and challenges for the field. Yet, there has never been a better time to look to the industry's thought leaders for insights, guidance, and clarity. How do security professionals successfully contribute to organizations in a VUCA world? A world that is Volatile, Uncertain, Complex, Ambiguous, and everchanging?

How do we Flip This Risk® ?

Enterprise security risk management is a holistic industry approach that takes a panoramic view of the risk and opportunity landscape; helping leaders look ahead.

Flip This Risk® for Enterprise Security provides a holistic snapshot of select security management issues. It is a compilation of stories from experts in the field providing unique and creative perspectives on several security management areas including risk and resilience, business continuity, executive protection, GRC (Governance, Risk and Compliance), global monitoring, and travel and event security.

In this book, our diversity of experts (who happen to be all women) provide powerful narratives from personal and professional viewpoints—creating an opportunity for readers to easily grasp the concepts that frame security management in organizations.

If you are seeking a better understanding of security management, desire additional knowledge about effective tools in the industry, or searching for leading practices that work in real-time—this book is for you!

- Use it as a guide.
- Use it as a reference.
- Use it for inspiration on your journey.

BRIDGET GUERRERO

Enhancing Your Organization's Resilience Through An Effective Corporate Security Program

"The Resilience Movement." We are hearing terms like this pop up all over the place today. Former US military Special Operations members are talking about the benefits of building personal resilience. Organizations are creating more roles to support operational resilience. In the corporate security domain, professionals are partnering with privacy, risk, and information security partners to build resilient organizations. What is up with all the talk about resilience? With one global challenge after another for the past year and a half, "resilience" is being viewed as a value driver. And if the intelligence forecasts hold, it looks like a topic we will continue to embrace for years to come.

Stepping off into adulthood as a US Marine Corps officer, I learned the value of "resilience" early. During initial Marine training, nearly every learning objective emphasized building, fostering, or demonstrating resilience. The nature of the job calls for individuals who can take the literal and physical hits and keep on fighting. Training opportunities include the concept of resilience, tests, and leadership messages.

Some Marines learn about resilience before the Corps through the realities of a tough life or on a less hefty scale through sports or academic rigor. Marines who internalize this value can withstand the challenges and quickly grow into strong leaders. Those who fail to thrive in this area are targeted and provided some extra opportunities to demonstrate resilience. If they show no hope, they are unlikely to be rewarded with the title of United States Marine. It is just that important.

After serving in the Marines, I put the concept of resilience into practice supporting the Intelligence Analysis division of the one-month-old Department of Homeland Security. Most are familiar with the "forming, storming, norming, and performing" organizational development framework. During those first few years of the Department, the organization "stormed" quite a bit and was challenged to transition to the "forming" stage. The Department was massive, the mission was unclear, and the well-known tools needed for my space, threat analysis & warning were unavailable. We had no formal intakes for threat information.

Still, we experienced an unmanageable deluge of threats coming in as the "See Something, Say Something" campaign kicked off without a well-mapped information management or threat management system behind it. A lot of committed people spent months of very long work weeks and weekends trying to create order. Small successes were realized despite the challenges. Working closely with the FBI, we created the first joint Homeland Security Information Messages and Bulletins. These products allowed us to share time sensitive threat information with critical infrastructure owners and the public. At first, the process was laborious- faxes going back and forth between government departments filled with red line edits from multiple entities. When dealing with national security threats such as terrorism, a sense of urgency accompanied our daily efforts, and time was of the essence. The lack of clarity of who was responsible for threat analysis and notifications slowed this urgent process to a crawl.

Fortunately, the people responsible for getting those communications out were used to working with ambiguity and uncertainty, and we pressed through to map analysis and review processes, production schedules and accountability matrices. Both Departments faced significant ambiguity and confusion each day. Still, teams continued to press to do the right thing out of a sense of duty to protect and an understanding that we could become better and more effective. Our endurance paid off and in turn, we contributed to the development of a more resilient organization with the Department.

We can synthesize some of the lessons learned from these early experiences to help inform on how to build resilience into corporate security programs. Enhancing an organization's ability to be resilient when facing adversity is a tremendous value add.

1. To start, understand your organization's view of risk. Too many security professionals define risk from their security-centered perspective. They invest time, energy, and organizational budget to employ controls to address or mitigate risks they perceive as most significant. Are these projects and goals aligned to the risks the business perceives as the most important? There are only so many hours in a day, and budgets are finite. Suppose you fail to build programs that address the critical risks of the company? In that case, you may not have the capacity, resources, or ability to confront these risks when they appear as threats to your company. It will not matter that you have built programs to address the risks you have assessed as most likely or impactful. If you failed to produce plans to address the business' perceived risks, you would have missed the mark.

Resilience professionals can tap into many sources to understand their organization's view of risk and the most concerning threats to business operations. A good start is to create a relationship with your Risk Officer or to find a way into your Business Continuity Planning sessions. Suppose your organization does not have a dedicated program to support enterprise risk management? In that case, you will have to find that information through your leadership or the Board.

You may also get helpful details through external analyses of your industry's most significant risks or the organization's audit results. Once armed with a more holistic view of your organization's view of risk, you can determine where those risks intersect with the security organization. Start addressing those risks, and you will catch the eye (and budget) from the top. Remember to speak this language with your leadership. Hence, they understand your strategy to develop programs that keep the business safe.

2. Anticipate and respond to threats. Building good ingests and sensor systems to quickly detect threats to your organization turns your team into a value-added partner.

Ingests are the feeds that deliver potential threat information to you. The information may come from human sources, global intelligence reporting, or automated notifications. Employees can serve as excellent safety and security crowdsource intelligence collectors. A recent Forbes article presented this issue well, stating, "In essence, frontline workers are the eyes and ears of an organization. They are the first to deal with others outside the business, and they are the first to interact with co-workers and contractors. This unique position enables frontline works to be ideal sources of intelligence, especially risk-related information for their company." [1]

The *sensors* include the active systems that scan the horizon to detect anomalies or problems, or the passive ones that alert to anomalies or issues. Sensors may include physical identity and access management platforms, camera systems, intrusion detection devices. It takes critical thinkers to manage these disparate systems today, so invest in the capacity and training of your teams that triage incoming issues. Train your teams to understand risk from the tactical perspective.

3. Methodically and quickly analyze impact. Systems may provide timely risk intelligence, but it takes skilled humans to promptly analyze how natural disasters, artificial disasters, or workplace violence impacts your employees, facilities, customers, or supply lines. Risk intelligence must be paired with contextual information to understand the timeline of the threat, the potential impact, and the immediately indicated mitigation. Open-source feeds, employees on the ground, and other data sets can also provide context. Building methodologies to provide context to these threats serves as a great aide to decision-makers.

If your Global Security Operations Center, SOC, or "911" center is in the United States and is responsible for assessing impact to global events, the ability to provide meaningful context may be challenging. Your credibility or your value as a security professional may be on the line if you do not assess context properly. It is a worthwhile investment to build out in-country support or contract with 3rd party intelligence providers to provide 24x7 support to the regions you cover.

If resources are an issue, you can develop your professional network to obtain valuable, quick feedback from experienced professionals operating in the same regions. Valuable resources include the Department of State's Overseas Advisory Council network, the Women in Security & Resilience Alliance (WISECRA on LinkedIn), or ASIS International. Your team provides value escalating the right stuff to the right people at the right time to mitigate risk. You must work hard to maintain that solid reputation.

4. Escalate the right stuff quickly. Escalations are dependent upon promising pathways and good relationships with your business partners. In most organizations, you will need to establish close relationships with many different business lines to support a resilient organization. For example, when working with threats of workplace violence, you may need to foster a daily relationship with one set of partners (Legal, HR, Communications, PR, Managers & Supervisors). For artificial or natural disasters, you may work with product lines, supply chain partners, regional teams, and a different set of HR, Legal, PR, and Communications partners.

In all situations, you may need to tap into external points of contact. The closer a relationship you have with these points of contact, the more supportive you can be in the manner and style in which you escalate potentially impactful event information. By knowing these leaders, you will also understand how they react to information and how soon they need to know about issues that may threaten the business. Help leaders understand that early information may not be accurate and that situations change as events unfold.

5. Who Does What During a Critical Incident?
Organizations vary in their business continuity management frameworks. Hosting workshops and regular planning sessions are critical for baselining critical event management and business continuity lexicons, job responsibilities, and processes. You will want to take time during these sessions to elicit an understanding of the leadership's escalation criteria. Larger organizations may have regional incident management teams and a separate, higher-level crisis response team. Enormous organizations may have entire structures dedicated to providing regional or business line support with little interaction between regions or business units. Some companies may create different teams who each specialize in a single type of threat. In contrast, others may operate a converged model, teaming up to address human threats to

the workplace, technology threats, and natural or environmental threats. However, your organization is structured, you will likely play a part in coordinating successful incident management protocols.

Regardless of structure, knowing "who does what" during a critical event is key to effective incident management. For several reasons, in smaller organizations, security teams frequently lead rather than support critical events. While the security team members may possess desirable leadership qualities to lead incidents as well as own several of the tools that can help the organization navigate a critical incident, a different business line may be more suited to lead the event. These issues can be worked out during those planning sessions.

A widespread problem experienced by organizations with emerging resilience programs is the lack of clarity of "who does what" during an incident. ITIL v4, a body of best-practice guidance for IT service management, addresses the importance of role assignment in incident management. This role assignment uses the "Responsible, Accountable, Consulted, Informed," or "RACI" framework to identify roles. When individuals know their roles and understand the roles of others, planning is precise, coordination is streamlined, and actions are implemented more quickly. That is resilience!

6. Help the Organization Return to Normal. Your team can provide exceptional critical incident coordination support to the business to help it quickly return to normal operations. Through mature detection and analysis protocols, your team can also notify leaders of "non-events," preventing unnecessary churn and stress on the organization. This comfort provides your business leaders the comfort and understanding they can then focus on other essential tasks, knowing you will notify them of any potentially impactful events.

7. Be Deliberate. Building resilient organizations make sense, but success may be hard to quantify. As you initially focus on building resilience, it takes "less doing" and more strategic planning to set your team up to effectively support this large task. The introduction to ISO 22316, a recognized body of knowledge that guides organizational resilience for any size or type of organization conveys it well. "Organizations can only be more or less resilient; there is no absolute measure or definitive goal." [2] Professionals need to take a strategic approach to building resilience. There will always be projects and opportunities to create a more resilient organization, so a focused and deliberate approach is most prudent.

8. Show your Work. Despite it being hard to quantify success at the macro level, there are several concrete ways you can demonstrate how your programs or teams contribute to a resilient environment. First, as you start incorporating good tools into your practice, you can demonstrate how many issues your team evaluates using a standard set of criteria versus the number of events escalated to incident or critical event level. You can report on successes related to improvements in how quickly you detect or contain incidents. Translate those improvements in time saved into a monetary value and you will catch the eye of the business leadership.

9. Lead well. Resilience requires robust and competent leadership. It is time for us to shed the old dialogue that security organizations are "cost centers." Learn to speak the language of the business and deliver results. There are innumerable ways to translate the value of safety, security, and resilience into cold, hard cash savings. Be a leader who is open-minded and creative. Take risks and experiment. And do not forget to be agile, as agility is a key to resilience.

Resilient organizations end up with a competitive advantage over organizations of comparable size and focus that have not made the people, process, and technology investments to develop resilient environments. The investment in resilience may not be obvious on a day-to-day basis but will pay off when it is critically needed. Just as Marines who are better equipped to take the hits continue to outperform others, a resilient organization will recover from events faster and lose its focus less often.

Your investments in resilience will allow business leaders to trust that your teams are managing the small events and escalating what matters. They can invest the time and energy in running the business knowing that when a significant event strikes, they will know who to turn to deliver results. Your team will be there ready to support the business, and that is a significant value proposition.

Bridget Guerrero is a certified business continuity professional with more than two decades experience supporting risk management, crisis management, intelligence and security operations in the United States Marine Corps, federal  government, non-profit, small business, and private sector. Bridget currently manages Global Security Operations & Resilience for GoDaddy and serves as the Vice Chair of the Overseas Security Advisory Council's Women in Security Common Interest Committee. In her personal time, she can be found participating in ultramarathon running and open water swimming events.

References:

1. Forbes, Guarav Kapoor, "The Frontline is your First Line Against Insider Threats," August 6, 2021
2. ISO 22316: Security and Resilience Organizational Resilience Principles and Attributes

RACHAEL TOVEY

What Is Business Continuity and Why Is It Important?

Business continuity (BC) planning is the ability to identify risks, plan for business disruptions, respond to events, and recover operations promptly. Businesses must prepare for a variety of disruptions such as weather events or more commonly now, cybersecurity incidents. Either event causes businesses to risk losing revenue, customers, and harm to their public image.

Business disruptions are occurring on what seems like a more frequent basis. Ransomware attacks, hurricanes, and ice storms are common news stories. Most recently and notably, the entire world has had to adjust its plans and means of operating due to COVID-19. Businesses with business continuity planning had to execute their plans and globally we all had transition to a new way of working.

Executives are critical to the success of a business continuity program. Without executive buy-in and support, widespread acceptance from business units is not likely to occur. Some people may find the planning stressful, and often, it is an added duty outside of regular work responsibilities. Once executives are on board with welcoming business continuity into the organization, they must be vocal and dedicated supporters of the program.

Where Does Business Continuity Fit?

The easy answer is wherever it makes sense for your organization. Business Continuity (BC) can align with Audit/Compliance/Risk, Security, or IT. For example, the best place for a bank's BC team may be under Compliance and Risk due to the regulatory requirements they must fulfill. To contrast that, a tech-heavy company may find it advantageous to include their Business Continuity team under the IT umbrella. Regardless of the department or division where Business Continuity resides, the C-suite and executives must realize the importance of a strong BC program.

Steps to Business Continuity Planning/Business Continuity Cycle

The first step in addressing business continuity planning is to conduct Business Impact Analysis (BIA) – this should occur at the business process level that makes sense for your organization. The BIA helps identify how long a business unit or process may not operate without impacting the overall business or corporation – the Recovery Time Objective (RTO). The BIA also includes assessing the operational, financial, compliance/legal, and reputational impacts if this team cannot operate over various time periods. For example, you may want to identify the reputational impacts to the overall enterprise at one hour, one day, three days, and one week. Additionally, during the BIA you should identify the criticality of the Business Unit, dependencies such as computer applications or critical vendors, and any mitigating factors, including inherent resilience, training, existing plans, or standard operating procedures.

One benefit of conducting BIAs is that executives have an overview of the most critical business processes and allow them to identify preparedness gaps and mitigation strategies that need to be addressed. Should a disruption occur, executives have the knowledge to prioritize which business units must be recovered first to minimize the overall impact to the business. This prioritization is critical to the overall organization and can aid decision-making in terms of funding budgets and identifying programs or strategies needed to reduce risks.

Once the BIA is complete, a Business Continuity Plan (BCP) is the next step. The BCP should address strategies to aid the business unit in responding and recovering from a business disruption. The standard BCP includes a method of recovery for loss of employees, loss of facilities, loss of critical third parties or vendors, and essential loss of technology. The BC planning team should assist the business owners in the process by including a template to complete, ensuring that BCPs are standardized.

After reviewing the BIA, it is easier to determine which parts of a plan may need more attention and work. For example, most companies had to pivot in 2020 from in-person office settings to working in a virtual environment. This shift presents a huge advantage to planning for a loss of facility. Similarly, in a company that relies on technology, such as banking or online retail, they may need to focus more on manual recovery strategies due to a loss of technology.

The H191 event in 2009 revitalized the need for pandemic planning to address the potential for loss of employees. Colonial Pipeline's ransomware event in May 2021 illuminates the need to plan for critical third parties and operations without employees. The gas shortage caused by the ransomware event resulted in airlines canceling flights, and other businesses felt the impact when employees did not have enough gas to get to work. This included businesses critical to the community such as grocery stores, hospitals, and pharmacies.

The planning sessions should be collaborative and include brainstorming. Ensure that people feel comfortable to speak up and share ideas. It may help to say, "Nothing is off the table. Be creative!" This planning potentially effects the future of the business – why limit ideas?

Some solutions may be simple. One example, how would your business continue to pay employees if there was an issue with either the payroll team or payroll software? Could you just pay employees what they were paid during a previous pay period and then manage any discrepancies once systems and teams were restored? Teams may have paper SOPs available but saving them on a secure shared site ensures access if needed from a remote location. A distribution center may be able identify a partner distribution center that can take over workload if one location is impacted. Moving from desktop computers to laptops can address the need for employees to be able to work from multiple locations.

During this planning phase, take time to document the roles and responsibilities of those people who will need to respond and recover to an event. Recommendations include assigning roles and responsibilities to a position, e.g., Vice President of Supply Chain or Senior Director of Human Resources, rather than a name. Then you can identify by name who will fill that role and their emergency contact information.

Training and Exercise

Now you have a plan, great! What next? A goal may be to write and include response steps. But this may not do any good if there is no training on what is in the plan. Anyone responsible for utilizing this resource should have training on finding it, accessing it, and what steps and procedures are included. They must also know what they are responsible for in the event the plan is needed.

One of the best ways to validate a BCP is to conduct an exercise. An exercise is a simulated event that allows participants a stress-free environment to determine what parts of the plan work and do not work and identify any gaps. Exercises should increase in complexity, starting with a tabletop exercise and escalating to a functional or even full-scale task.

Exercises can be simple too! One of your identified risks could be intermittent power outages, and your recovery strategy is to have a backup generator. If the generator is already on-site, practice switching over to the generator for power. If you do not have a generator on-site, procure one and ensure you can hook it up and switch power over. Now is a great time to check and make sure there are contracts in place to secure the generator, especially in locations prone to weather events.

Another exercise could be using the manual procedures for technology recovery strategies to make sure they work. Have a team work through a simulation using the manual techniques that would be implemented in a technology outage. Make certain people have alternate logins to email and know how to access shared documents.

Encourage employees to work from home periodically. We have all learned from the past year that going into the office is not always a possibility. Working remotely can help prepare employees so they know where and how to access shared files. The business can verify that it has the network and VPN capability to accommodate a larger than normal population to work off site.

Once the training and exercises are complete, and gaps are identified, now is the time to update response and recovery strategies in the business continuity plan.

Real World and Lessons Learned

Exercises are great for practicing and running through a plan; however, real-world events offer another excellent opportunity to verify the plan that addresses everything needed for an effective response. Even if your organization is not impacted directly or significantly, make the most of any opportunity to test your plan.

Other Strategies

As you work on business continuity, you may realize that you will end up with cross-functional plans. Even though it's a daunting prospect, your organization will end up more prepared for disruption.

Ransomware and cybersecurity attacks are on the rise. Often an organization's entire network is unavailable. How will your teams work together to ensure that you can still operate on some level? Health care systems have been a primary target, and Universal Health Services suffered an attack in 2020. All systems were unavailable, and doctors and nurses were charting on paper. Medical files, prescription information, patient charts were all unavailable to hospital employees. These are organization-wide disruptions that would require a cross-functional plan.

Resources

ISO 22301 was developed and published by the International Standards Organization. The document outlines the basic elements of a program. It can be a valuable document to consult as you start or build out your business continuity program. ISO 22301 defines terms and concepts necessary to develop your program. The standards are also revised, updated, and expanded periodically so new concepts and requirements are integrated into existing standards.

Join local planning organizations, security organizations, work with other private sector businesses, and share ideas. Sharing ideas, benchmarking, and building relationships are invaluable. Conferences provide another outlet to exchange ideas and learn new processes.

Ensuring that your company or business is ready and prepared for operational disruptions can be intimidating. However, as an executive, you are responsible for helping identify and mitigate risks to the success and longevity of your company. Business Continuity planning is integral to identifying and planning for those disruptions.

Rachael Tovey is an experienced Business Continuity and Emergency Management professional with fifteen years of experience. Rachael started off in the public sector working for North Carolina Emergency Management and then segued to the private sector world. Her experience in the private sector realm includes working with Fortune 500 entities. Rachael has held positions with the National Emergency Management Association, served as a representative on the Department of Homeland Security Healthcare and Public Health Sector Coordinating Council and Department of Homeland Security Commercial Facilities Subsector Coordinating Council, and is a member of the International Association of Emergency Management.

BARRIE BURREN

Executive Protection

What is executive protection? It is more than men in suits and sunglasses with earpieces. It is keeping someone safe. There are different approaches, but before getting started, it is essential to recognize that there is no such thing as total safety. There is a world out there that people live in, and whether intentional or by accident, bad things can and do happen.

Executive protection entails providing services to support the safety and security of an individual with an increased risk profile. This function encompasses identifying and mitigating risks to an individual through planning, implementing risk-reduction measures such as enhanced monitoring and situational awareness, and executing a swift response to identified threats.

At its core, executive protection is identifying and mitigating risks and being aware of tradeoffs.

Who can apply this?

Anyone can be subject to a safety or security threat. That is why planning, taking common-sense security precautions and maintaining situational awareness—all included in this chapter—prove valuable practices for all. However, some individuals carry a higher risk profile and require a higher level of protection. That is where executive protection comes in.

How many guys in suits do I need?

Before answering the question "how many executive protection agents (the men characterized as bodyguards wearing suits in the movies) do I need?" many factors must be considered, namely what is the risk profile of the principal (the person you are protecting)? Someone with a high net worth may be at risk of being exploited for their millions but unrecognizable to most of the public. A pop singer may be at risk of being swarmed by fans when venturing into public. Someone without money or previous fame but currently at the center of an emerging scandal may require executive protection for the first time until the situation blows over.

That is to say: a risk profile depends on the person and the scenario. The same person may require various levels of protection based on location and circumstances. For instance, a high-powered executive will not need as much protection when staying on remote family property outside of the spotlight compared to attending a large-scale event after announcing that their company is making a change viewed unfavorably by critics. Staying tuned in to ever-changing circumstances is an essential first step toward making sound executive protection decisions, including determining an appropriate number of executive protection agents.

Who does what?

Since executive protection is about matching security measures to the threats, there is not a one-size-fits-all approach. When selecting an executive protection team, you will need to determine the roles of the individuals involved in the executive protection detail (the security word for "assignment"). For instance, will all executive protection agents accompany and blatantly swarm your principal? Hopefully not. Part of the planning process entails ensuring individuals are on-site looking for potential threats before your principal arrives, then meeting the principal and accompanying agents upon arrival.

The sharing of information across this team and other parties involved in security – whether law enforcement or venue security – is critical. Understandably, you will not want to share every piece of information. Usually, a need-to know-basis is at play, but proper coordination with trusted parties can maximize the web of individuals supporting your principal's security. Comparing a security assignment to a children's soccer game, if the principal is the ball, you cannot have every agent chasing after the ball; the approach requires creating plays ahead of time and assigning roles. This balanced approach also leaves a few cards up your sleeve. Keeping a few agents at a distance (and not requiring everyone wears a suit) can build a more discrete approach to executive protection.

What risks might I encounter?

Does what we have covered so far sound like common sense? The good news is that, in many ways, it is. The more difficult news to swallow is that we can get in our own way. Still, you are (mostly) in control of what you put forward.

Below are a few common risks and guidance for overcoming them.

Not planning for the more likely threats

Call it catastrophizing, call it the influence of Hollywood, whatever you call it, recognize that many people immediately turn to the worst-case scenario. Yes, it is a good idea to prepare for anything, but focusing efforts on the threats seen in the movies creates a risk of failing to prepare for the more likely situations. For instance, the likelihood of being in a car accident or suffering a medical emergency is far higher than being kidnapped. So, prepare for everyday emergencies. Ensure the executive protection team trains on first aid and CPR. If your principal has a medical condition, equip yourself with the necessary medications.

The lesson: Focus efforts on planning for what is more likely to happen, even if it is less likely to become the next action thriller.

Not planning for contingencies

Using provided information, you may plan a great security detail. However, life throws curveballs, and it is your job to prepare for them. Suppose the assignment is to transport a principal across a rural but dangerous area securely. If you are a top-notch executive protection agent and you hire a security-trained driver, you might think your work is done. But what if the car that is being used gets a flat tire and there isn't another car available to be deployed for more than an hour? Your principal becomes a sitting duck. You may not have expected the car to get a flat tire, but the trouble is always plausible if a vehicle is involved. Your job entails planning for contingencies. Consider what could go wrong, hope it does not happen, but be prepared if it does. In this scenario, have a backup vehicle, along with a backup agent and driver, available to deploy at a moment's notice. Better yet, if the budget allows, send the second car close behind.

The lesson: Make a great plan A and make a great plan B (and beyond).

Thinking you are in charge

Yes, you led planning efforts and are prepared to take charge, but it is important not to confuse that for being in control. If you are providing security for an influential person, be honest with yourself that they are in charge. In executive protection, your job is to plan, prepare, mitigate risks, and advise. Leaders may overrule you, and your advice might be heard but not followed. How could that happen, you might ask? Security is the most important thing! For one, most people believe their job is the most important thing. The person in charge of Public Relations, for instance, might think that the risk of your principal not making an appearance at a particular event is more likely to have terrible repercussions than whatever security threat you foresee.

For another, sometimes the principal changes their mind. For instance, although you planned for what was intended to be a straightforward trip, while in the car, the principal sees a part of town that must be explored. The vehicle pulls over, the principal exits, and you are now traversing an area that you have not completed an advance on (meaning that you have not checked out the site ahead of time to familiarize yourself and clear it of threats). In these circumstances, you may need to gently remind the principal the danger but go along with it, taking the precautions possible as you adjust. Ideally, you reviewed the area thoroughly when planning, selected a route that avoided areas with the most significant threats, and have some familiarity with the location you now exploring.

The lesson: Prepare to be flexible and incorporate changes into your planning.

Creating something that will not be followed

Have you ever started making a great backup plan only to fail with the execution, like making a spare key but storing it inside of your locked home? Implementing security measures for your principal can present some of the same challenges. For instance, you can identify and install a state-of-the-art security system for your principal, but they may forget to arm it or find it too complicated to use. Either way, it becomes ineffective. Part of your role is helping your principal recognize that taking a few seconds out of their day for a security-focused task can yield meaningful results for their safety. Another part of your role includes learning your principal and understanding tradeoffs.

For instance, if a security system is slightly less perfect but your principal gets excited about and understands how to arm it (and therefore will use it), it is a far better solution than the alternative. Alternatively, your principal may experience protection fatigue and crave time when they do not feel a security presence. If you continue to push numerous close protection agents on them, you risk scenarios where the principal stops sharing vital information or backs away from security in a big way. Instead, it is better to scale back the approach to their comfort, like having an agent at a distance or offering to check an area before they visit. After all, some security is better than none.

The lesson: Listen to your principal and match the security measure to the person.

Missing the obvious

When immersing yourself in every focused detail, missing the apparent presents a serious risk. For instance, you may have poured over the placement of sensors and cameras for your principal's security system.

But if your principal's son posts a video on social media and the video happens to show someone entering the code to disarm their system, an essential piece of data is compromised. Or the risk could be less obvious, like the principal's daughter proudly sharing a photo of her new vehicle, which reveals the license plate number.

Or perhaps the principal's spouse decides to hire a new gardener without conducting any checks, which would have showed the "gardener's" direct grievances with the principal. An innocuous action can quickly breach a strategically crafted approach to security. Often this comes from the misunderstanding that the responsibility of security resides solely with paid security staff. It is important to educate the principal, and all involved about the actions that they must think through and to drive home the understanding that security is everyone's responsibility.

The lesson: Instill in others a personal sense of responsibility for security.

How do you measure success?

Now that you understand some of the risks and challenges associated with executive protection, let us take a moment to consider measuring success. Ideally, successful executive protection does not involve making a big tackle to take down a bad guy headed for your principal. Rather than measuring a day's success in statistics (14 bad guys apprehended, three quick escapes, and a partridge in a pear tree), a good day in executive protection lacks Super Bowl-level excitement.

This is because comprehensive planning and a hint of luck prevented threats from manifesting or because your approach quietly mitigated the threat. Whatever the reason, a "boring day" is often a successful day, especially when you consider the consequences. A mistake in this space does not lead to a missed touchdown; it could lead to grave danger to another human being.

Still, some executive protection folks do not mind a bit of excitement now and then because it reminds the broader team around the principal that security is a real risk. Even if executive protection teams quietly thwart risks, it does not mean they are absent.

At its core, executive protection is an opportunity to consider an individual's risk profile, personal preferences, and the presented scenario to thoughtfully create plans, implement appropriate security measures, and provide for their wellbeing.

Barrie Burren is a strategic communication and global security professional. Looked to as a thought leader, Barrie believes engagement drives progress. Her efforts focus on process, effective organizational design, and buy-in.

CANDACE McCABE

Governance, Risk and Compliance (GRC)

This chapter will introduce you to the area known as Governance, Risk, and Compliance (GRC). We will discuss the various disciplines included in GRC, potential organization structures, and familiar stakeholders. We will demonstrate a set of questions to help you evaluate the potential risk to determine if that risk is acceptable and how. We will also introduce some of the risks that each function may face and demonstrate how these disciplines may work together for cross-functional risk management to promote business outcomes.

What is GRC?

If you do not know what GRC is, do not feel bad. You are not alone. When the group of contributors to this book met the first time, one of the contributors asked, "What do you mean by Governance, Risk, and Compliance?"

GRC is a set of capabilities that encompass several different disciplines or functions within an enterprise. There is no singular definition of what GRC includes or does not include. The purpose of GRC, however, is standard. GRC's mission is to build and manage policies, processes, and standards designed to minimize enterprise risk while promoting business outcomes. GRC is the set of functions designed to provide a balance between profit and risk.

The GRC acronym refers to:

- Governance – Standard, policies, processes, and procedures designed to enable risk management and compliance
- Risk – Identification, evaluation, and mitigation of enterprise risk
- Compliance - Establishing legal, regulatory, and ethical business practice controls

The GRC discipline may be a centralized or decentralized function. Each enterprise's organizational structure can vary. Part of GRC will fall within the Finance, Legal, or Technology departments within some organizations. Some of the groups in the GRC scope may include:

- Asset Management (Software/Hardware)
- Disaster Recovery
- Records and Information Management
- Information Privacy
- Data Governance
- Audit
- Vendor Management
- Worker Health and Safety
- Legal Support/ eDiscovery
- Change and Program Management

These disciplines will share the responsibility with familiar stakeholders. Typical internal stakeholders for any GRC organization will include Information Security, Internal Audit, Finance, Legal, and Technology. External stakeholders may have shareholders, customers, suppliers, and the public-at-large.

What types of risks do you manage within GRC?

While they may remain under a standard heading of GRC, each discipline has its own set of risks to consider and potential opportunities. Leveraging risk mitigation processes helps to achieve better business outcomes. The primary risks for each area are specific and mitigating the risks within each area requires specialized focus.

For example, IT Asset management's primary focus may be on licensing, ensuring that the organization complies with software and hardware usage standards, meets capacity and contract terms. While managing compliance with contracts, IT Asset Management may also note capability overlaps between software packages or underutilized assets. Renegotiating better contract terms or eliminating redundancies to save money in licensing fees will be an option.

The Vendor Management discipline will primarily be responsible for making sure that vendor contracts are standard and favorable. Vendor Management practices involve ensuring that system access by contract workers is consistent with the work they perform. But still, follow auditing and documenting access best practices. This area will also focus on ensuring proper financial controls regarding the vendor selection process, invoicing, and payments.

Change management is responsible for ensuring that technology or process changes are thoroughly tested and approved before being introduced into a production environment. Often, change management processes are evaluated in terms of regulatory compliance, where processes or systems are related to financial reporting or human resource management.

Disciplines within the GRC umbrella often work together to develop mutually beneficial risk mitigation strategies that can support business strategies such as cost reduction. Records and Information Management, Information Privacy, and Data Governance may set standards for records and information retention. Minimizing privacy risks aids the Legal Support/ eDiscovery function by reducing the volume of documents and information in response to legal action. The IT Asset Management function may also work closely with Information Security to manage versions or patches for the latest security standards. Internal Audit will work very closely with Change Management to develop standards and processes that are fully auditable to comply with financial regulations.

How is risk in GRC evaluated?

To evaluate risk in this space, as in many others, you should ask yourself a set of questions. Answering these questions will help you analyze the potential reward associated with an acceptable level of risk. Your organization can develop mitigation strategies and compliance practices to minimize the cost side of the equation.

The first question to ask in any risk evaluation is, "What's the worst thing that could happen?" It is not a question meant to be flippant or sarcastic. Instead meant to provoke you to think through the absolute worst-case scenario. Be realistic in your answer and consider potential costs regarding sanctions, fines, litigation, loss of revenue, or reputational damage. For example, corporations have seen share values decline following a public data breach on average 7.5%.

The second question to ask in your risk evaluation is, "What's the best thing that could happen?" Again, be very realistic in your expectations. Where possible, use quantitative measures such as revenues, return on investment, or days to process. In addition to quantitative measures, qualitative measures such as customer satisfaction, brand loyalty, or trust will give a better perspective of the benefits of accepting and mitigating the risk.

Once you have answered the worst- and best-case scenario questions, you will need to assess the likelihood of each of these scenarios and the possible timeframe in which each could occur. For instance, if your worst-case scenario involves litigation that is of moderate likelihood within five years but low likelihood within 1-3 years, but your best-case scenario is highly likely within 1-3 years, you will need to determine if the potential cost outweighs the potential benefit within that 1–3-year range. You are looking to pick the tipping point on the scale within a given period at this stage. This evaluation will determine what costs you are willing to accept to ensure that the benefits outweigh the risks.

The next question is key to determining how to proceed in your risk evaluation. At this stage, the question to ask is, "What can we do to weigh the outcome in our favor?" Are there controls, processes, systems, or people who can help reduce or eliminate the risk factors and realize the benefits? What are the costs to implement the strategies, and how can we minimize those costs while ensuring that the strategies are effective? What are the controls to implement immediately, and will require investment or time? How much investment is needed?

At this stage, you are looking to determine the tipping point on the scales. This evaluation will determine what costs you are willing to accept to ensure that the benefits outweigh the risks. Once you have thoroughly examined and documented the risk and reward factors and a cost-benefit evaluation, you will be able to identify where the tipping point is in your risk plan. Often, a set of controls and processes can eliminate much of the risk while allowing the organization to capitalize on the benefits.

How is compliance ensured?

When you were a child, "because I said so" was the explanation used for compliance with a directive. Today, you will understand that simply publishing a policy and expecting the enterprise to adhere to it is not realistic. In the past, organizations would create policies and standards without the inclusion of the groups required to comply with those same policies and standards. Those groups may or not have had the ability to voice objections, pose questions, or suggest changes. They may have complied in part or in whole out of fear but would be more apt to follow the letter, rather than the spirit, of the policy.

Collaborating with stakeholders and achieving buy-in is the best potential solution to compliance with risk management strategies, particularly in the GRC space. Implementing governance frameworks to support a policy and identifying means of ensuring compliance requires that you work with all stakeholders. The stakeholders contribute to, understand, believe in, and support the governance and compliance functions' standards. It would be best if you worked with these groups early and often. They will be able to articulate what is, and is not, possible, or likely.

Governance and compliance organizations are known for saying, "No." It is time to change that reputation. GRC professionals need to work towards saying, "Yes, And." That change of language puts GRC in partnership with the groups that are moving towards business outcomes while managing the risk in the programs, processes, or technologies that the groups are desiring. In addition to changing the language of the conversation, it is vital to bring in other constituents to contribute additional ways to mitigate risks. You can gain multiple perspectives on mitigating those risks while realizing the maximum benefits.

For example, your chief data scientist thinks that his team can build a unique customer view that will lend itself to process automation which will speed up your sales cycle and increase revenue. The team has projected a 25% reduction in time and a 5% increase in revenue through this new modeling. The team is extremely excited about this prospect and is ready to charge forward.

While the Data Science team is looking to expand the business goals, GRC groups may address concerns. The Privacy team may be concerned with the increased volume of PII stored within the models. The eDiscovery team may worry about retaining additional data, which requires policy changes and potentially increases eDiscovery time and cost due to contained data. The Information Security team is likely to need to develop other safeguards for this data set.

To manage the risk, rather than saying "No" to the Data Science team, look for the Win-Win and say, "Yes, and." In this scenario, work the Data Science team to consider anonymizing the data to reduce the privacy risks and eliminate the eDiscovery concerns. Have the Data Scientists collaborate with the Legal team to develop bias and fairness tests for the data sets and the model outcomes. By encouraging these groups to work together, the enterprise will leverage risk management for a product that achieves the business objectives without negatively impacting risk.

There are often other opportunities that cross-functional boundaries. For instance, a new market for the enterprise may have unique health and safety regulations that require the development of new standards, processes, and technology capabilities. The investment in developing these new capabilities could then be leveraged as a competitive advantage in an existing market with lower regulatory standards.

Risk management in the GRC space enables the business objectives while reducing risk to an acceptable level within reasonable mitigation costs. The policies, standards, and frameworks created to ensure compliance with risk management are the purpose behind all GRC organizations.

Candace McCabe, CIP, is a strategist, architect, and thought leader in Information Privacy, Governance, Enterprise Architecture, and Technical Architecture. Candace is passionate about Information Privacy and Digital Ethics. She  regularly speaks publicly on topics in the Governance, Risk, and Compliance space. Candace is also a leader, advocate, and ally for diversity in STEAM education and careers. Candace can be reached via email at arinfogoverness@gmail.com on Twitter @arinfogoverness or LinkedIn at https://www.linkedin.com/in/candacefotimccabe

DANIELLA BOVE-LaMONICA

Risk and Resilience

The term *resilience* has become a corporate buzzword used to describe scenarios ranging from an individual employee's capacity to manage personal adversity to an entire market's ability to withstand force majeure events. At its very core, *resilience* involves constructive and effective adaptation to change. To that end, we can define o*rganizational resilience* as an organization's ability to sustain adversity and recover from challenges that would seek to disrupt its people or operations.

The concept of organizational resilience, particularly as it applies to the modern corporate security/risk function, was redefined in the wake of the September 11th terrorist attacks. The attacks showcased, in horrific glory, the level to which the United States underestimated both the innovative capabilities and the destructive drive of the threat actors working against the country. The collapse of the Twin Towers generated shockwaves through corporate America.

CEOs, aghast at the collateral consequences of terrorism, turned to internal security professionals to help make sense of what would, ultimately, be the new corporate normal. Painstaking analysis of the event has revealed that, regardless of the unimaginable scope of the catastrophe, there was an apparent lack of security preparedness and training on numerous fronts which compounded the lethality of the disaster and unnecessarily contributed to loss of life.

Beyond the tragedy of the day, there are numerous stories of 9/11 heroes that improvised their way through the chaos to save the lives of others. There is also one standout example of effective organizational resilience: a unique corporate security program unprecedented for its time, particularly one in a property as complex and seemingly impervious as New York City's World Trade Center.

Between 1997 and 2001, Morgan Stanley's headquarters at the WTC occupied twenty-two floors of the South

Tower and security was under the remit of Rick Rescorla, a highly decorated Vietnam Veteran turned corporate security professional. Rescorla was known throughout the company as a dogmatic believer in preparedness and had been outspoken with senior leadership about the significant physical security vulnerabilities of the World Trade Center site.

In the wake of the 1993 bombing in the Trade Center's parking garage, Rescorla launched a vehement campaign to have Morgan Stanley move its operations to New Jersey, to somewhere with a lower profile and fewer operational liabilities. Simultaneously, Rescorla, unimpressed with the safety posture of the NY Port Authority (who owned overall security at the site), established enhanced evacuation protocols for Morgan Stanley employees.

When the first plane hit the North Tower, and despite Port Authority announcements for tenants to remain at their desks, Rick Rescorla ordered his employees to head towards the stairwells. By the time the South Tower was hit, Morgan Stanley was already in the process of evacuating the building. Rescorla's focus on adapting his company's security posture, his drive for organizational resilience in response to what he saw as a clearly evolving threat landscape, saved 2,687 lives. Sadly, Rick Rescorla perished in the collapse of the Second Tower, but his work has contributed to high-rise security reform and his legacy remains a source of inspiration to the corporate security profession.

Post-9/11, most companies integrated specific internal functions to develop comprehensive risk mitigation frameworks, taking a holistic stance on corporate resilience. Such frameworks are an integral component to creating a more resilient organization because companies that fail to manage risk inherently damage their operational stability. It is important to remember that risk related to resilience, whether at the individual contributor or functional group level, can be identified and managed but never really resolved. The mitigation of "resilience-related risk" is a unique task, intrinsically a continuously moving target, defined by a landscape perpetually in flux.

Acknowledging that a firm's goal should be a long-term, organization-wide approach to resilience and risk management, any enterprise mandate should not preclude developing departmental risk mitigation strategies. In laymen's terms, individual teams should focus on mitigating risk as it relates to their specific business line or operational requirements, regardless of whether an all-encompassing corporate risk strategy is a stated objective of the company.

The focus of this chapter is the creation of risk-related resiliency within the corporate security function.

Creating a Resilient Security Organization

A corporate security team's definition of operational resilience and how it assesses its internal resilience risk is a very nuanced, bespoke process. There are no blanket solutions as multiple variables affect how a company cultivates and maintains its internal security function. That said, there are understood best practices that will help mitigate resilience-related risk within a corporate security group.

Understand that risk-related resilience is multi-functional and multi-faceted.

It is essential to promote an infrastructure that is mindful of resilience-related risk. A firm's resilience is only as good as the weakest link in its risk mitigation chain. Moreover, many organizations have internal biases which inhibit or distort the effective management of risk. Numerous internal organizational blind spots, particularly expert group silos, could potentially undermine the team's resilience posture within the security function. Silos can be functional, operational, cultural, and behavioral and present in some combined form.

Creating a balanced approach towards resilience is critical to minimize a silo mentality within the security team and engagement with stakeholders. An excellent practice to counteract silos or bias is through the engagement and involvement of multiple practitioners and stakeholders. Through collaboration, norms and assumptions can be challenged and vetted, which bolsters the entire firm's risk mitigation posture.

Develop a risk profile.

A resilient security team is vigilant about the risk landscape facing its host organization. A robust risk profile incorporates strategic and behavioral elements which best reflect where and how a firm position's itself within a more extensive market context. The construction of this profile should not be done in isolation by the security team-- a group typically limited to managing the physical, geo-political or digital risks within its purview. A comprehensive product will include input from other functional areas such as operational risk, legal, compliance, human resources, information, and technology. It will consist of tripwires for group activation based on a criteria consensus. A successful assessment will evaluate internal and external risk factors of significant impact as well as the mundane.

In short, big-ticket items such as terrorism, pandemics, and natural disasters need to be considered alongside callouts for lack of capacity or the loss of internal expertise. If possible, the profile should include quantitative elements to compliment any qualitative assessment. Once a profile exists, the product owners should regularly convene, embracing a proactive posture that allows the functional areas to assess whether mitigation updates are required due to ongoing internal and external monitoring and analysis.

Have a playbook.

A playbook, loosely defined for this chapter, is a set of assessment criteria and related reactions compiled to assist a team in establishing a set of response parameters. A team playbook should include benchmarked best practices relevant to specific concerns and be comprehensive enough, yet tightly edited for operational ease, to serve as a stand-alone document. Playbook training and testing via real-time scenario exercises should be mandatory and scheduled on a frequent enough basis to ensure familiarity. In creating a training and testing schedule, the team should also evaluate the potential merit of ad hoc testing, though unexpected scenario training typically only benefits teams with a certain level of internal maturity.

The security team should also bolster the resilience capacity of stakeholders and other functional counterparts by exposing those entities to the relevant materials on a regularly scheduled basis, reinforcing the currently available corporate tools, resources, and processes. Ongoing, expanded playbook training and testing programs serve several additional purposes: they are a pathway to receive feedback and manage expectations. Engagement also helps test and vet operational assumptions via scenario exercises and assists in risk mitigation by exposing potential gaps or flagging previously unseen warning signs.

Take every opportunity to invest in and enhance resilience competitiveness.

It has been proven that resilience offers a competitive advantage within any given marketplace. Security teams that prioritize resilience will find increased operational stability and effectiveness as a result. In seeking out where to invest time, training, and resources, intangibles such as leadership and culture should not be ignored. Certain studies have mapped the success patterns of "high-reliability organizations (HROs)." Places like hospital emergency rooms, nuclear plants, and aircraft carriers must cope with disruption ranging from the trivial to the extraordinary. Despite the diversity of operations, these industries have specific cultural commonalities.

Teams working within an HRO environment are trained to prioritize flexibility, act with anticipation, and defer to expertise. HROs practice crisis management during business-as-usual daily activities as well as during incidents of impact. HROs have a strong tolerance for uncertainty and have expanded abilities to absorb low-grade strain on the organization without sacrificing operational effectiveness. A successful tactic also employed by HROs is to train and maintain additional resources in case surge capacity is required. Corporate security teams should invest in resources that assist with developing a similar mindset to optimize resilience. A competitive, risk-resilient squad is trained and prepared to act on multiple fronts while reserving the room for improvisation.

Establish recovery priorities.

Restoring essential business services and mitigating operational disruption is only one part of a recovery campaign. Any resumption of business should be seen as merely a baseline objective after a disruptive event. Like those within the HRO environment, a resilient team takes the opportunity presented by a crisis to explore lessons learned and build capabilities accordingly. Stakeholder management, training and testing provides the corporate security function with a key avenue to reinforce resiliency expectations for the aftermath of an event. Best practices suggest that teams hold a "postmortem meeting" as a key part of any recovery strategy. Such a meeting ensures there is time for an "after-action" review among stakeholders where elements of the crisis can be discussed at length, assumptions challenged, and feedback shared. These review sessions are invaluable to improving the team's resilience posture as they drive future organizational infrastructure investments.

Conclusion

In 2003, a group of researchers published a paper examining frameworks for creating disaster-resilient communities as part of earthquake preparedness and response. Within the qualitative and quantitative presentation, the team inaugurated the "four Rs of resilience" (Bruneau et al., 2003). The framework outlined four critical characteristics to resilience success: robustness, redundancy, resourcefulness (agility), and rapidity. As corporate security teams look to mitigate resilience-related risk, teams should embrace the 4R concept as they build out each element of their resilience program.

Keep in mind:

- Embracing a **multi-faceted approach** to resilience means ensuring capabilities are robust and with some level of redundancy.

- Involving stakeholders beyond security supports creating resilience work products, like the **risk profile**, which are creative, effective, and adaptive.

- A tightly honed **playbook** that is vetted and routinely tested is a guarantor of rapidity and robustness of response.

- **Investing in resilience capabilities** allows for increased agility and capacity in mitigating risk.

- Setting **a clear framework for incident recovery** and incorporating stakeholder feedback will ensure a more robust, more risk-adaptive resilience posture moving forward.

Daniella Bove-LaMonica is a corporate security practitioner with two decades of experience spanning both the public and private sectors. Beyond her current security role, Daniella is a published author and

speaker, a tenured fellow with the Truman National Security Project and is currently pursuing a Doctorate in Organizational Leadership at Pepperdine University. She can be reached on LinkedIn at www.linkedin.com/in/dbovelamonica.

End Notes

Bruneau, B., Chang, S., Eguchi, T., Lee, G., O'Rourke, T., Reinhorn, A., Shinozuka, M., Tierney, K., Wallace, W., von Winterfeldt, D. (2003). A Framework to Quantitatively Assess and Enhance the Seismic Resilience of Communities, Earthquake Spectra 19:733-752

Gould, David. (2018). Organizational Resilience Approaches to Cyber Security. International Journal of Smart Education and Urban Society. 9. 53-62. 10.4018/IJSEUS.2018100105.

Jones, Bernard., D.Sc. Benchmarking Organizational Resilience: A Cross-Sectional Comparative Research Study. (2015). Mentored by Dr. Michael Chumer. 200 pp.

National Commission on Terrorist Attacks Upon the United States. *The 9/11 Commission report: final report of the National Commission on Terrorist Attacks upon the United States.* [Washington, DC: National Commission on Terrorist Attacks upon the United States: For sale by the

Supt. of Docs., U.S. G.P.O, 2004] Web. https://lccn.loc. gov/2004356401, Chapter 9, 278-323

Stephenson, A. (2010). Benchmarking the resilience of organizations (Doctoral thesis, University of Canterbury, Christchurch, NZ). http://www.resorgs. org.nz/Publications/

Stewart, James B. "The Real Heroes Are Dead." *The New Yorker,* vol. 159, no. 6, 11 February 2002, https://www.newyorker.com/magazine/2002/02/11/ the-real-heroes-are-dead

Tierney, K. J. (1997). Business impacts of the Northridge earthquake. Journal of Contingencies and Crisis Management, 5(2), 87–97.

Weick, Karl & Sutcliffe, Kathleen. (2007). Managing the Unexpected Resilient Performance in an Age of Uncertainty. 8.

SONIA TRAVI KNOWLES

Global Monitoring and Response

"Gotta risk it for the biscuit, mamma! But have you figured out your risk tolerance yet?"

had been observing the John Hopkins map since December and dreading the time when COVID-19 reached Latin America or Africa. My concerns were based on their tolerance for something I could see could have significant health, economic and social impact. Even though I planned a short trip the following summer, I never really imagined the length of this Pandemic, how it shaped geopolitics or the effect it would have on my risk tolerance.

In the security world, we know that it is all a matter of time before an impactful event happens, so being two steps ahead is vital. By monitoring global events and being aware of global geopolitics, one can move forward. Even if not forecasting events' timeframes accurately, one can have an educated guess over possible outcomes. Awareness increases resilience, and in the end, one of the main goals of a Global Security department is to increase organizational resilience.

On March 12, 2020, as we drove to the airport to catch our Istanbul flight, all travel was suspended to and from Schengen countries. My first stop before entering Turkey was in Vienna, and it also was our return pit-stop. Unfortunately, due to COVID-19, the executive decision was to cancel the trip. I did not have a security plan or contingencies for a pandemic situation. Suddenly, my risk tolerance on a scale of 1 to 10 was 0.00, so I drove home to re-assess, re-engage, and act. I ended up in Cancun for a weekend, but that is for another story.

I grew up in a country filled with terrorism and was taught how to be calm, think, prepare, and respond to threats pragmatically from an incredibly early age-from sheltering in place to kidnappings. Before heading out anywhere, I had to leave three points of contact. If you recall, cellphones in the 1980s-1990s were not accessible.

I had to have a MEET point for pick up and drop off (and no, you cannot use the same place twice) and research the location to confirm the emergency exits and possible threats. To   this day, I rather sit next to and face the emergency exit with my back against the wall.

I guess you can say that risk mitigation was an everyday lesson from a physical security point of view. The love for history and geography came later, and I would find that two things are critical in Global Monitoring and Security with time. From an early age, I was made aware of my risk tolerance.

The monitoring of global events supports effective business continuity. It helps to understand risk tolerance at an individual level, which involves active awareness and honesty with oneself. At an organizational level, it helps businesses engage in business with a certain level of knowledge that permits optimal resilience. At this level, things can get complicated because we are now talking about safeguarding and helping business units maintain optimal standards: Supply chain timeliness, effective operations, personnel, and asset security.

Monitoring global events allows organizations to accept and improve their risk tolerance because they also prepare for contingencies. The remarkable thing about observing international incidents and connecting possibilities is how awareness improves timeliness in response. It is about when IT will happen, instead of if IT will happen: Observe, Prepare and Act.

Global Monitoring for a Security Professional

A merge of Global Monitoring for the Security Professional ends up being: Global Security. I am sure that someone, somewhere, has already coined the term but to be fair, Global Security is, in the end, what the organization wants it to be. Do they want to monitor global events to increase personnel and traveler's safety? Perhaps improve business continuity? Enhance internal resilience mechanism? Regardless, each organization has different needs, and these can be effective with an appropriately trained security team. A team can connect geopolitics with localized emergency management and protective intelligence.

A global security professional is responsible for observing, analyzing, connecting, and hopefully forecasting events that will directly or indirectly affect the resilience and business continuity of the organization. Likewise, it has the responsibility to remain neutral while empowering risk-owners with the knowledge to face and hopefully overcome hazards.

Global monitoring and response are related to how security professionals analyze risk indicators, observe events, react to them, and help build resilience. Yet, what is an acceptable level of risk?

Observing and monitoring incidents (such as weather, economic and political stability, corruption, natural disasters impact) is influenced by perception, often a unique perception, so it is essential to remain neutral in all assessments. Monitoring events is not about having an opinion - unless it is used to forecast- on defining who is right or wrong but offering the stakeholder a complete view of the events to decide what is best for the organization.

Business Risk

0.0	Political Stability
0.0	Economic
0.0	Corruption/Bribery
0.0	Natural Disasters
0.0	War

| 0.0 | Business Risk Rating |

If one forecasts possible outcomes, it is imperative to present the historical, political, cultural, and religious background of the region and country and a brief historical background of similar events, so those ingesting the information can understand the difficulties they encounter may face. For business operations and to support successful business endeavors, this is key. Resilience is built with knowledge.

Global Security in Travel

Because I grew up traveling, I understand – firsthand- that it offers as much education and knowledge as time in the classroom, so I budget for two international trips a year with my boys. While growing older, I let my eldest make a list of the countries he wants to visit and a few reasons why he wants to go there. In such a way, I get him to see the importance of history and how geographical locations can impact safety. He must list at least one incident (and mitigation) that could make our trip dangerous.

In 2019, he picked the summer of 2020 in Uganda with lions as the highest risk and Turkey for Spring Break, with earthquakes as the highest risk. To emphasize, he has the mind of a 10-year-old.

My job is to teach my little risk-owners to see around the corner before they get there. As it happened with me while growing up, I know they need risk mitigation tools similar (less intense) to those I was offered. Additionally, because they are my weakest link, increasing their resilience means I grow my own. I become the organization.

When it comes to corporate travelers, increasing their resilience increases the organizations' too. The traveler must understand the cyber and physical risks when traveling and have a general sense of how things operate wherever they are headed. Let us call it cultural and business awareness. I believe in empowering risk owners with this knowledge and being part of any business continuity plan. In both examples (my children and the average corporate traveler), the risk owner is empowered with awareness and guidelines on mitigating high-risk situations.

So far, I know that my kids will not accept packages from strangers at an airport's bathroom (and yes, this happened once). Instead, they will run outside that room screaming as loud as they can yet, not all travelers have that level of safety and security awareness. My little travelers started young. So, when it comes to making corporate travelers the risk owners, I have a process.

Travelers need to understand that they are the risk owners, and the organization can only offer them mitigations tools. They are responsible for their safety. If their Travel Security department or Global Security Operations Center provides the information, then it is up to them to ingest it and understand it. For example, a Country's Risk Profile. Many private and public organizations offer risk levels for regions and countries.

My favorites are The British Foreign & Commonwealth Office (FCO) and the Department of State, alongside some well-known for-profit organizations.

Through a Country Risk Assessment offered by a third-party vendor or built   exclusively for the organization), I let travelers understand the independent indicators within the Country Risk Profile. Then I describe how to self-assign values to certain personal situations. These are assigned on a scale of .01 to 5.0. The higher the number, the higher the risk. When the risk owner gives values, these will self-tabulate alongside the Country Risk Profile to offer an overall Travel Risk. These areas are shown in the tables below.

Country Risk Profile

0.0	Terrorism and Crime
0.0	Medical and Transportation
0.0	Social Unrest and Political Stability
0.0	Natural Disasters
0.0	War

0.0	**Total Country Risk**

The risk owner must assess a Personal Risk Profile. Did they read the Country Risk Assessment or researched the location's cultural, religious, political situation? What are their physical (property loss) risks? Will they travel with valuables? Where will they safeguard these? Will they attract attention? Do they need any medication? Maybe their medicine is not legal at their destination. Or what about LGTBQ travelers or females with children traveling alone? Will they be staying at their hotel or venturing out for activities? Do they have emergency contacts set up?

Expatriates are a special group because they require specific training to reduce activity-related risks, especially at HIGH-RISK locations. I have discovered that this group tends to be accepting and resilient by nature. As a former military spouse, I can relate to them and see them as assets within any organization.

Personal Risk Profile

0.0	Pre-Travel Assessment
0.0	Individual Risks
0.0	Travel Awareness
0.0	Activity Related Risk
0.0	Emergency Contacts

0.0	Total Personal Risk

Most importantly, what about the risk owner points of contact and emergency contacts? Do they carry copies on their cellphones? What is the backup if they lose their cellphone and bag? A security professional's job is to help risk owners be mindful and self-aware as they prepare to travel. I had a family get robbed, ending up with zero access to emergency contacts except one, their company's 1-800 number to the Global Security Operations Center (GSOC) imprinted on a keychain. Gladly, the GSOC was a point of contact, and they had access to their passport numbers, emergency contacts, and other pieces of information.

Travel Risk Profile	0.0

When it comes to Global security and monitoring and helping travelers build resilience, Murphy's law also applies: Whatever that can go wrong will go wrong. One must always be ready.

Perception and Awareness

A few years ago, I took my eldest child, a student attending one of the first Arabic Immersion Magnet schools in the United States, to the Middle East. He was not only my translator but also my "risk-tolerance" compass. Despite the amount of cultural, political, religious, and knowledge over proper social behavior in that region, I perceived myself as vulnerable. I was traveling with a child to an area with volatile risk ratings as per the analyses of various international organizations and did not speak Arabic.

As an analyst, I started to use perception and awareness to measure risk and help people understand their risk tolerance. Security professionals are responsible for empowering risk-owners with knowledge so their decisions become less harmful to themselves or their organizations.

Awareness intensifies resilience, and in the end, one of the main goals of Global Security is to reduce risks and increase stability.

When thinking about risk, the risk-owner must prepare for threats by accepting vulnerabilities through awareness. Awareness from a perspective of knowledge will help them decide while in distress. When it is necessary to be hyper-aware (an exhausting process), a good example is my kid running out of the bathroom when asked to carry a package to the plane, and there are also times when one can relax and enjoy. In other words, wherever there is a risk, one must be aware of what is happening around to make decisions that will help increase tolerance and reduce risk exposure.

Through the monitoring of events globally, individuals and organizations can assess their risk tolerance. Each individual and each organization is different, but all of them need security professionals that will provide them, through assessments, with the proper level of awareness to improve their risk tolerance.

What is your risk tolerance?

Insignificant	Low	Medium	High	Extreme
.01 -1.0	1.1 -2.0	2.1 - 3.0	3.1 - 4.0	4.1 - 4.8
I	L	M	H	E

Sonia Travi Knowles - With over 10 years of experience in protective intelligence, travel security and emergency management, Sonia Travi Knowles calls herself a "one-woman GSOC". She was a government contractor for  several Intelligence Agencies and Law Enforcement organizations, before moving into Corporate Security in 2014. Travi-Knowles is currently in Houston, developing and implementing Global Security Operations Centers. She graduated from Texas A&M and is pursuing an MBA in Global Management and Virtual Organizations.

She also has several graduate certificates in Emergency Management, Project Management, and Social Media Management/Intelligence.

Although she is passionate about her professional life, her primary focus is her children. She travels with them internationally at least twice a year and gains energy from seeing them explore the world. In her words: "I would never advise anything to anyone if I were not comfortable doing it with my own family."

RITABETH CRAGUE & SHERRY TUCCI

TRAVEL AND EVENT SECURITY

In a globalized economy, business travel is necessary for companies of all kinds and sizes, which creates the need for a robust travel security program. The purpose of having a corporate travel security program in place is to protect both the company and the employees that travel to all corners of the world on the company's behalf.

Travel Security

Crime, accidents, medical emergencies, delays, and inclement weather are daily occurrences worldwide, but the added element of travel can compound the impact for an individual. International travel presents more significant risks than domestic business travel because it takes the employee out of a familiar context and away from customary medical and security resources.

An unfamiliar environment—and language barriers—can make responding to even a minor event significantly more difficult. The goal of a travel security program is to assist an employee in responding to events and minimize negative impacts for both the individual and the company.

Leaders should tailor a travel security program to the corporation it serves, but all travel security programs have common factors. An effective travel security program covers aspects of travel before, during, and after the trip. Critical components of a business travel security program include a country risk rating methodology, pre-travel security assessments and briefings, travel emergency services, the ability to locate employees while traveling, and post-travel debriefs.

Duty of Care

The concept of Duty of Care encompasses ethical and legal responsibilities a company has for the wellbeing of its employees. In the US, business travel is covered under OSHA regulations to provide a safe work environment. The legal obligations vary from country to country, but a business travel security program should be designed to cover all the applicable legal responsibilities.

Pre-Travel

Fortunately, most of the legwork is done before the traveler even embarks on their journey when it comes to business travel security. Pre-travel preparations equip the traveler and the supporting security team with awareness and tools to respond to potential security events. The process begins with assessing the risk associated with the business travel itinerary, usually focused on the destination(s). Assigning risk by country is the most common risk assessment method, though analysis can also be conducted at the city level, depending on travel scope.

Most risk methodologies use a three or five-level scale: low, medium, and high; or low, moderate, medium, high, extreme. It is up to the organization to decide what each risk level means, though they should directly correlate with the security requirements a traveler must fulfill to undertake the travel. The range can be from little beyond the pre-trip briefing for low and moderate destinations to the necessity of secure ground transportation and an increased check-in frequency for high and extreme risk itineraries.

There are a variety of resources for establishing a risk rating system. Examples include third-party security vendors, government and open-source assessments, and an in-house travel security team analysis. The primary considerations for risk ratings are the threats of crime, terrorism, civil unrest, and kidnapping; geopolitical concerns and political instability; and destination infrastructure (quality and availability of medical services, quality of roads, hotel, and hospitality services).

Risk ratings should be reviewed regularly to ensure accuracy. It is also helpful to have a process to account for sudden changes in a risk environment, such as a breakout of mass civil unrest or significant military escalation. When addressing these events, it is essential to designate who is responsible for proposing risk rating changes, who is responsible for approving the changes, and who is responsible for communicating the changes to travelers.

With a risk rating system established, security teams can better understand how best to assess the associated risk of a traveler's itinerary. From a traveler's point of view, pre-trip preparation begins with engaging with the security team for an itinerary review. For travel to higher-risk countries, it is crucial to understand where precisely the traveler will be going, where they will be staying, how they will get around, and when they will be moving about. With a thorough itinerary review, security teams can make appropriate security recommendations and arrange security accommodations.

For example, travelers going to remote locations may need secure ground transportation or an aviation review for sites that are only accessible by helicopter or charter plane. For travelers working overnight, the security team should assess the crime risks and areas to avoid while abroad. And in general, it is always important to review for planned protests, potential disruptions due to national or religious holidays/events, or recent security incidents near a traveler's hotel.

A pre-travel briefing email is sufficient to provide business travelers with relevant security and awareness information in many cases. For high and extreme risk destinations—or VIP travel—security teams may consider providing verbal briefings to allow travelers to ask specific questions. In both cases, in addition to destination-specific and general travel security information, briefings should include details of the company's emergency travel resources and contact information for the responsible security personnel. Many travel security programs also incorporate pre-travel security awareness training.

During Travel

With all the pre-trip assessments and briefings out of the way, the travel should proceed smoothly, barring any sudden events. Security teams typically have a 24/7 operations center or GSOC, with analysts monitoring for any disruptions at all hours of the day. Global monitoring is an essential function of a travel security program, albeit a bit boring at times – the good news is, the more boring, the better (for the traveler at least!) However, when a security event does occur, managers should communicate those incidents to business travelers.

As a result, one of the most important abilities for any security team is to quickly locate employees on business travel and provide them with resources and support. Most corporate business travel security programs use a vendor to track travelers and provide alerts tailored to their destinations.

Whatever method is used, it is a best practice to have some mechanism to provide updated alerts to travelers about events near them that could impact their travel. These could include inclement weather, traffic disruptions, civil unrest or protesting, or criminal activity and applies to international and domestic travel. An employee is still in an unfamiliar location in either case, so the travel security team is acting as an extra set of eyes and ears for the traveler.

Another thing to consider is an established check-in system for those going to higher-risk locations. These check-ins can be conducted via phone, text, email, or other means (ex. a specific vendor app with a check-in capability). After an itinerary review in the pre-travel stage, security can work with the traveler to create a check-in schedule to meet security's needs and work for the traveler, including a primary, alternate, and backup communication method. Travelers should also provide emergency as well as local business contacts for alternate contacts in-country.

For example, a traveler going to India might have a nightly check-in via email at the end of each day for the week they are on business travel. A missed notification will alert the security team, who can then take steps to establish contact. The first step would be to call the hotel and ask to be connected to the traveler's room – usually, this can solve the problem, such as if the traveler is experiencing a wi-fi or connection issue.

If that does not work, security should follow the contact tree established with the traveler before departure to confirm the traveler's status. In the meantime, the traveler should also follow the selected communications plan and attempt to contact the security team using an alternative or backup method, such as a phone call or even messaging a family member to make contact on their behalf.

In most cases, a minor communication disruption like dropped wi-fi will be quickly discovered and end the escalation process. In the event of an actual security threat, having established check-in windows gives a security team the advantage of acting as quickly as possible and taking the right calls to action. The best practice is for travelers to issue their final check-in when they begin their return. For rail or car trips, travelers should check in when they start their return journey. For flights, this would be when the traveler is checked in and passed security for their return home.

Emergency Response

Companies should ensure that they have the appropriate resources to assist a traveler in an emergency while on business travel. A Business Travel Accident insurance policy typically includes the benefits and coverage necessary to address most business travel-related issues, such as travel assistance services (lost luggage, passport) and emergency medical expenses. Companies should also consider including coverage for political and natural disaster evacuation, repatriation of remains, and kidnap and ransom events.

A travel security manager can develop an emergency response plan to reference in a significant security event.

The plan should include contact information of the people involved in emergency response, such as essential business leaders and internal stakeholders from HR and Legal teams, regional security contacts (if applicable), and relevant policy numbers and security vendors.

Post-Travel

A post-travel process allows business travelers to provide feedback about their trip and alert the travel security manager to any gaps in the program. Some companies conduct an annual survey of business travelers, while others send a post-travel study after every trip. Whatever the method, travel security managers should assess their company's business travel risk posture on at least an annual basis to identify trends and ensure their travel security program has adequate resources based on the risk exposure from business travel.

As a rule of thumb, managers should not just assume that any security incident during travel will be reported to them. There are many reasons why a traveler may not register an incident, large or small, that could range from embarrassment to nonchalance – or it was just because they were never asked! Outreach after a trip can make an enormous difference in receiving feedback.

Event Security

Corporate events pose temporary security risks that combine elements of travel security and daily business operations. One can think of event security as parallel to travel safety in terms of having a beginning-middle-end type of process; however, while travel can happen daily, significant events can be exceedingly rare. As such, each event may be handled uniquely based on the circumstances.

As with travel security, a pre-event assessment is a foundation for event security planning. The assessment includes the site and a review of the risks posed by the attendees and planned activities. A shareholder meeting that is closed to the public but headlined by a CEO is vastly different from an outdoor music festival where alcohol will be served. Using the assessment, a security manager can develop mitigation strategies for access control, guest safety, and adequate staffing. In all cases, open communication and good contacts with the relevant local authorities are recommended.

When conducting the pre-event assessment, security teams should also consider any potential backlash or negative response toward the event. For example, a shareholder meeting may attract protestors opposed to a company or its activities. Major sporting events may also carry risks of rowdy demonstrations by passionate fans either celebrating a victory or denouncing a loss, which should be considered for post-event security.

On-site security plays a significant role in monitoring for any threats during the event and responding as appropriate. As a result, event security planners should verify that event staff has the relevant training necessary for their areas of responsibility, such as crowd control and alcohol compliance. Before the event, all staff should be well-briefed on their positions and duties to keep activities and attendees safe and secure.

A post-mortem review is helpful to capture lessons learned and improve future event security planning. Those involved in security event planning should consider what aspects were successful and review any security incidents and responses to identify gaps in the event security plan. These lessons learned can be incorporated into future event planning or used for a post-event briefing or presentation.

Conclusion

At a high level, travel and event security share many similarities and are straightforward once processes and procedures are developed. The most crucial aspect of any travel or event security program is a focus on prevention and preparation. While it is impossible to avoid every potential security incident, having an established travel or event security program allows security teams to respond confidently to events and protect their company's personnel, property, and reputation.

RitaBeth Crague is an IOSH certified Travel Risk and Security professional with over 15 years' experience in risk management and security analysis. Ms. Crague currently works as a Travel Security Manager and Geopolitical Risk and Intelligence Analyst for Lumen Technologies.

Sherry Tucci is a young security professional with experience in travel security, global intelligence, and incident response. She has a background in journalism and currently leads a 24/7 team of GSOC analysts. Outside of  security, Sherry is a black belt in taekwondo and has competed internationally in Olympic-style sparring.

TRAVEL SECURITY PROGRAM CHECKLIST

Below are key components to consider when building a travel security program.

Pre-Travel

- A risk rating method for travel locations
- Pre-travel security assessments and awareness briefings for travelers
- An itinerary review

During Travel

- A business traveler location system
- A communication process for travelers to alert the company if they need assistance
- A mechanism to monitor real-time events tailored to business travel itineraries
- A Travel Security Manager or team who regularly reviews security alerts and contacts impacted travelers when appropriate

Emergency Response

- An emergency response plan for travelers who need assistance.
- A Business Travel Accident (BTA) policy. Coverage should include emergency medical resources,

security evacuation services, and repatriation of remains

- Kidnap and Ransom coverage

Post Travel

- Business Travel Program metrics review and analysis
- Business Travel Program Traveler Survey

8

KAREN HARDY

Conversations with Leaders:
Developing a Strategic Mindset

Developing a strategic mindset is critical for security professionals. It can also be a challenge to acquire when your core skills are the focus. The following interviews provide insights about strategic value and how any security professional can establish it within their organization.

Interview with Steven Antione, former Chief Security Officer (CSO) at YUM! Brands* discussing the importance of defining strategic value for security professionals. This is an annotated excerpt from the podcast interview on January 19, 2021.

Dr. Karen Hardy: Thank you, Steven for being a guest on the podcast. Given your public service and military background, how has that influenced what you do now as a Chief Security Officer (CSO) and how you manage risk within your field?

Steven Antoine: Well, it is funny because it is not intuitive. When you are making the transition from public service to corporate service, you find that corporations may not want former police or military. From the environment where we come from, where it is law enforcement and rule enforcement, the focus tends to be mitigating risk, avoiding risk, or accepting risk. Well in corporations, you can always leverage it. That is no different than what I did before: trying to leverage risk.

I think in how we look at risk taking now, the question is, well, what is our risk tolerance as an organization and what are we trying to accomplish? Because the risks to me are the things that get in the way of us being successful of the goals that we set forth as an organization. That is how I define the risk. Not so much the traditional bad guys and geopolitical unrest, though all that stuff matters. But only in the context if they get in the way of what we are trying to achieve organizationally.

Dr. Karen Hardy: People often ask how do I define risk? Or what is the definition of risk?" I just put that right back in their lap because you must define that for yourself. Agree? Disagree?

Steven Antoine: Absolutely agree. That is fluid because when you are a support mechanism in an organization that has been successful or multiple organizations that has been successful, people like to think that you are going to come with a certain lens, gates and guards and you are not going to understand the macro business. That hill is a steep one to walk. The sooner that you can illustrate that you are plugged into the overall mission of the organization and that your job is to enable it by addressing the HOW, not the "NO, YOU CAN'T DO THAT"—the better.

Risk comes with opportunity. We must frame it that way. So, I absolutely agree that I do not determine what the risk tolerances are. Leadership does and that helps us then better frame how we can support.

Dr. Karen Hardy: How do we define value? Now I have my own perspective. Value is hard to sell, and it is based on one's internal belief system. You really need to find out what your stakeholders value first, and then put on top of that value system the practice of risk to protect it.

Steven Antoine: Well, that is exactly it. What do they value? Then how do you support and protect the things that they value is how we define our value. You are right. It is fluid. I think that the other part of that is -- it is a journey. It is a journey because only someone else can determine what success looks like. When you are a support mechanism, they say, "Okay, success to us means it's based in M and A. We're going to acquire X number of organizations and we're going to move in this direction." Well, if that is what success looks like, our job is to enable that to occur. How do we get to yes? We are only successful if they accomplish what they have set out to do.

Dr. Karen Hardy: How do you elevate security to a point where it is making a difference strategically within organization, because it is not unusual for organizations to comprise of silos. The challenge is elevating that siloed mentality to one that impacts the macro-organization.

Steven Antoine: It is a tough journey. I invited myself to meetings. I would show up in meetings, trying to figure out how our business partners and our stakeholders think, and what is important to them.

Dr. Karen Hardy: Physical security has been a topic of interest during the pandemic. How do you get to the table?

Steven Antoine: They need a bigger table, but it is also incumbent upon us not to cry wolf all the time. We must remember that what we do a hundred percent of the time matters to your organization 1% of the time. We must put the appropriate lens and passion behind the appropriateness of the issue because if we scream about everything, you will get disregarded, and you will never get invited to the room because they are talking about growth in multiple countries, and you are focusing on access control.

Dr. Karen Hardy: Is security part of the strategy versus only being called upon to "fix" an immediate problem? Because I have seen that happen, where you are brought to the table by leadership as fixers, but you are not part of ongoing strategy.

Steven Antoine: You're right. That is why the enterprise risk management piece comes in and gives them an insight into a lens of all types of risks that can inhibit organizations from getting to where they need to go without those tribulations in between if it is leading into the right direction. ERM is designed to help bring to the level of attention what those cross-cutting risks are within organizations and then a leadership needs to make decisions about those. As security professionals, we need to get out of that classical training. We must understand the greater context of the business itself and where, what we are trying to put in place protects them from what they value as important. So, when it comes to asset protection, well, what assets matter? What are we trying to protect? Is it information? Is it people, is it function?

Dr. Karen Hardy: What's on the horizon for the security field?

Steven Antoine: We're not unlike any other business or any other function. People are trying to figure out how do we stay connected in a place where people are much more remote where there are challenges in putting people in the same space in groups. We are trying to figure out how to evolve and to stay relevant and to become more relevant in some instances, to contribute on a macro level, to all types of industries. How to broaden out our skillsets, where we can cross pollinate, and how do we partner in spaces and places where we did not normally show up.

---

*YUM! Brands has over 52,000 restaurants in more than 150 countries, primarily operating the company's brands such as KFC, Pizza Hut and Taco Bell.

Interview with Paul Godfrey, Professor of Business Strategy, Brigham Young University*

A lot of the companies that I work with, I do not think do as well as they should. A lot of times the overriding question is, "how will this play out over the next three months? How will this play out in this quarter's earnings in the next two or three quarters?" And good companies start asking question number one: "Is what we're thinking about consistent with our mission? Is it who we want to be?"

And then number two, they start to ask, "if we go down this road, will we be in a position that will really create value for our customers over the long-term that will be a great place for our organization to grow and thrive? Will it be sustainable?" Can we keep it going over several years so that the investment has time to pay off?"

Far too many organizations and companies are concerned about quarterly profits, and government organizations are concerned about next year's budget cycle. There are so many short- term pressures that crowd in on us that it is easy to not think strategically.

*Annotated Excerpt from the Flip This Risk Podcast interview, August 2020

NOTES

Afterword

Thank you for supporting Flip This Risk® for Enterprise Security! Flip This Risk® Books focus on and is committed to three core elements:

1. Diversifying thought leadership in the risk management literature.
2. Simplifying complex information for broader application.
3. Creating smaller, environmentally friendly books.

We are proud of the experts who committed their time and energy to make this book a success and to take on this professional development project to become published thought leaders!!!!

It is especially exciting because this is the first FTR community book written **entirely by women!**

It is time for a new conversation about risk management, resiliency, and leadership.

And it is a global conversation-- all the way from the boardroom to the barbershop down the street.

Everyone is invited to the table.

Our work is just beginning.

Please encourage our authors. Follow them on social media. Purchase their book and leave reviews on Amazon.

Thank you again for joining us on this journey and for being a part of the Flip This Risk® community!

ABOUT THE AUTHOR

 **D**r. Hardy is the CEO of Strategic Leadership Advisors LLC which is dedicated to helping organizations maximize their performance and remain resilient.

Dr. Hardy's career includes experience at the White House Office of Management and Budget, Executive Office of the U.S. President, and building an enterprise risk management function at a $7B public sector agency from the ground up.

She is a two-time bestselling author and recipient of the Most Promising New Textbook Award. She was inducted into the National Academy of Best-Selling Authors.

Her book on risk management reached #6 on the Amazon Top 100 List for Risk Management. She is also creator and host of the award-winning Flip This Risk

Podcast, where she interviews high achievers about their relationship with risk-taking and how it influences their leadership resiliency.

She is the co-author of *Mastering the Art of Success* with Jack Canfield (creator of *Chicken Soup for the Soul*) and co-producer of the four-time Emmy Award-winning documentary, *A New Leash on Life: The K9s for Warriors Story*, a film about the risks of veterans with PTSD. The film can be seen on Amazon Prime and PBS stations.

You Can:

- Email: drkarenhardy (at) yahoo.com
- Follow on https://www.linkedin.com/in/ drkarenhardyspeaks
- For speaking inquiries visit https://www.DrKarenHardySpeaks.com
- For consulting/training services, visit calendly. com/drkarenhardy to schedule a 15-minute consultation.
- Subscribe to FlipThisRiskPodcast.com

SPECIAL ANNOUNCEMENT!

To Learn More About Our Book Writing Program,
visit **bit.ly/AuthorOpportunities**

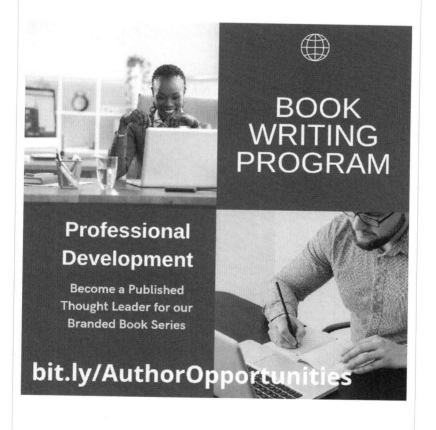

Made in the USA
Las Vegas, NV
01 April 2022

46683815R20063